HOW TO DRAW
CUTE ANIMALS

This book belongs to:

Daphne

HOW TO DRAW CUTE ANIMALS

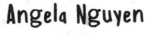

Angela Nguyen

STERLING CHILDREN'S BOOKS
New York

STERLING CHILDREN'S BOOKS
New York

STERLING CHILDREN'S BOOKS and the
distinctive Sterling Children's Books logo
are registered trademarks of Sterling
Publishing Co., Inc.

ISBN 978-1-4549-3101-0

Distributed in Canada by Sterling Publishing
c/o Canadian Manda Group, 664 Annette
Street, Toronto, Ontario M6S 2C8 Canada

For information about custom editions,
special sales, and premium and corporate
purchases, please contact Sterling Special
Sales at 800-805-5489 or
specialsales@sterlingpublishing.com.

Manufactured in China

Lot #:

2 4 6 8 10 9 7 5 3 1

07/18

sterlingpublishing.com

MIX
Paper from
responsible sources
FSC® C104723

CONTENTS

—— THE CUTE CREATURE COLLECTION ——

Hi there, my name is Angela!

I'm an illustrator who is known for cute drawings, especially of animals. Animals are so dynamic, cuddly, and fun to draw, and cute animals always make people happy.

I have collected together some of my favorite creatures to show aspiring artists, like you, how to draw them; now you can follow the steps I have and complete the activities I have created for each critter.

I'm excited to show you these very special home, farm, forest, jungle, safari, and water animals! Whether you're a beginner or the best artist in your group of friends, join me on this cute journey and learn how to draw adorable animals.

TOOLS

There are many types of tools you can use in this book. The key thing to remember is to choose a marking tool that will not leak through the page! I suggest you check your pens on a separate sheet of paper first, to make sure you can't see any marks when you turn the paper over. These are the tools that I love to use.

The pencil is a go-to!

PENCILS
Pencils are ideal for sketching and creating fun textures. Pencil marks are also easy to erase if you make any mistakes.

PENS
These are my favorite! Pens are great when you want a thin stroke. You can get precise drawings, like small paws or little whiskers.

Be bold with a marker.

Sharpies define lines.

Metallics add sparkle!

There's no going back with a pen.

Don't forget to put a cap on your markers after drawing with them so they don't dry out.

CRAYONS
If you're going to be doing a lot of coloring, crayons can be a fun tool to play with. They make interesting textures and thick strokes.

Use art markers for rich color and vibrancy.

MARKERS
Markers can be a bit risky because they are ink heavy, so test them out first. I have some markers in my office that are light and create beautiful thick strokes.

Try not to drop colored pencils because the lead inside will break.

Colored pencils are great for shading.

BASICS OF CUTENESS

You can adapt these simple steps for drawing any animal.

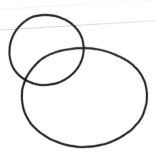

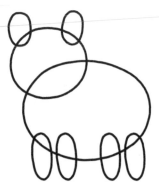

STEP 1: THE BASE
Most animals will be made of two circles: a small circle for the head and a large circle for the body. Depending on each animal, the two circles might be closer or farther from one another.

STEP 2: LIMBS
Limbs are fun! They stick out of the body in whichever direction you choose. Depending on the animal, you can make the limbs shorter or longer. Animal ears also come in all sorts of shapes.

STEP 3: TAIL
Some animals have a long tail, while others may not have a tail at all! Imagine that Step 3 is similar to Step 2: it's like adding another limb.

STEP 4: DETAILS
Once you have the basic anatomy of your animal, you can fill in the details. Add fur, a face, patterns, and everything else that will bring your animal to life!

This deer has too much detail.

Much cuter!

1 SIMPLIFY
By focusing less on the details you can concentrate on cuteness! Use fewer lines and simple strokes for all your animals.

2 LIGHT COLORS
Use pastel colors to lighten your animals. Intense colors will make your animals look too serious (unless that's what you're going for!).

3 ROUNDNESS
Round shapes like circles and curves will ease the eye. They make your animals look friendly! Look how chubby I made this giraffe.

ANIMALS ALIVE

Try a dotted path to show where your animal is walking.

Draw straight lines coming out from the face. Surprise!

Action lines are special effects you can add alongside your animals to animate them. Bring your animals to life with a few extra pen strokes.

Curved lines can show that your animal is happily bouncing along.

Wavy lines are most effective for underwater creatures. You can show which direction this stingray is swimming!

You can add all sorts of fun special effects, like hearts, sparkles, or sleepy "z"s.

Straight lines give this tiger speed!

You can tell this dog is wagging its tail because of the small curved lines I drew.

FACIAL EXPRESSIONS

Change the shape of the eyes, eyebrows, and mouth to show how your animal is feeling. Here are some ideas for you.

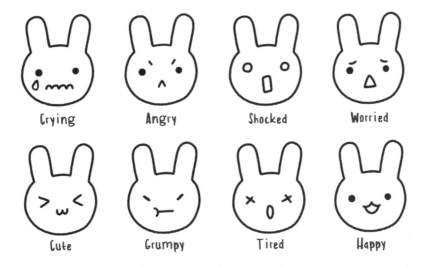

Crying	Angry	Shocked	Worried
Cute	Grumpy	Tired	Happy

THE **CUTE** CREATURE COLLECTION

18 HAMSTER

20 DUCK

22 HEDGEHOG

24 CAT

26 FOX

28 MOUSE

30 RACCOON

32 RABBIT

34 DOG

36 COW/BULL

38 GOAT

40 SHEEP

42 PIG

44 CHICKEN

46 HORSE

48 WOLF

50 BEAR

52 KANGAROO

54 DEER

56 OWL

58 ARMADILLO

60 LLAMA

62 BAT

64 KOALA

66 RED PANDA

68 CAMEL

70 DINOSAURS

72 MONKEY/GORILLA

74 COLORFUL BIRDS

76 ELEPHANT

78 HIPPO

80 GIRAFFE

82 LION

84 TIGER

86 SLOTH

88 LIZARDS

90 LEMUR

92 RHINOCEROS

94 FROG

96 WHALE

98 DOLPHIN

100 FISH

102 PENGUIN

104 OTTER

106 SHARK

108 CRAB/LOBSTER

110 STINGRAY

112 SEAL

114 SEAHORSE

116 WALRUS

118 OCTOPUS/SQUID

120 NARWHAL

122 BEAVER

124 TURTLE

126 PLATYPUS

HAMSTER

Hamsters love seeds, nuts, raisins, fruit, and corn.

Hamsters are nocturnal and love to run around at night.

Nom nom nom. Hamsters like to stuff their mouths with food. Draw some hamsters enjoying a feast of different foods. Don't forget to fill up their bowl.

DUCK

A mallard has a green head and looks like it's wearing a white necklace.

Ducks have flexible necks that can turn and rest on their backs.

Remember that drawing baby animals is like drawing smaller adult animals!

I drew a giant mama duck for you. Now it's your turn to draw her ducklings swimming closely behind her. After drawing, what colors will you use for the whole family?

HEDGEHOG

There are about 5,000 to 7,000 spikes on a hedgehog, but you don't have to draw that many!

I like to start the hedgehog with a silhouette. Then define where the back and belly are with a line.

When you draw the belly of a hedgehog, begin with a round shape.

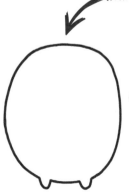

Did you know that hedgehogs like to take baths? They can float on their backs and tread through water. Draw your own floating hedgehogs, with water lines around them.

CAT

There are many things cats like: toys, string, food, catnip, napping, and grooming.

Yarn

Mouse toy

Catnip

Fish

Cats spend a lot of time just lying around.

Practice drawing different tails on these
cute kitties. Try a fluffy tail, a straight tail,
a short tail, and a curvy tail.

FOX

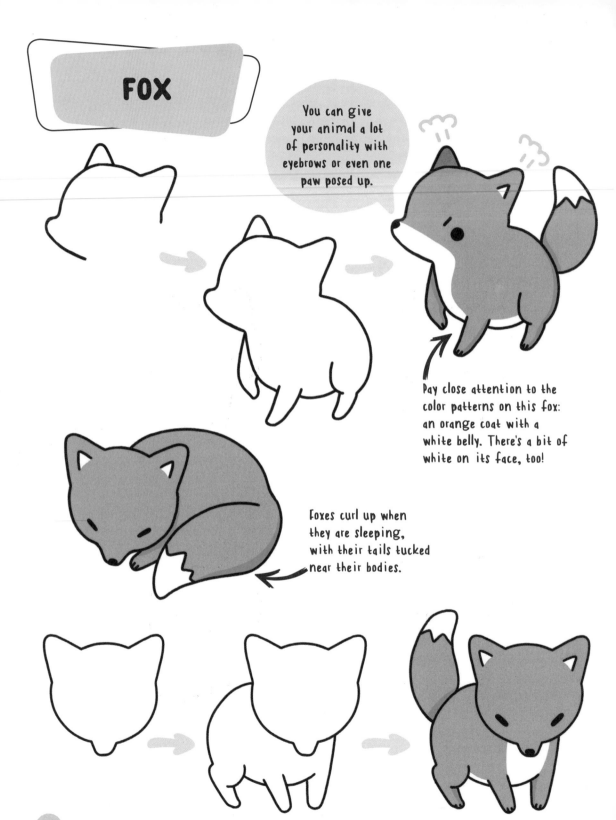

You can give your animal a lot of personality with eyebrows or even one paw posed up.

Pay close attention to the color patterns on this fox: an orange coat with a white belly. There's a bit of white on its face, too!

Foxes curl up when they are sleeping, with their tails tucked near their bodies.

Foxes like to dig holes and crawl into burrows for food. This fox is peering into a stash of snacks it has collected. Draw the hole he has dug, filled with lots of food.

MOUSE

Nom nom! Give your mouse a piece of cheese to munch on.

This little mouse is busy washing its face.

Mice can crawl quickly and swiftly, and sneak up behind you!

Draw a little mouse peeking out from its home in the wall as it smells the yummy cheese snack.

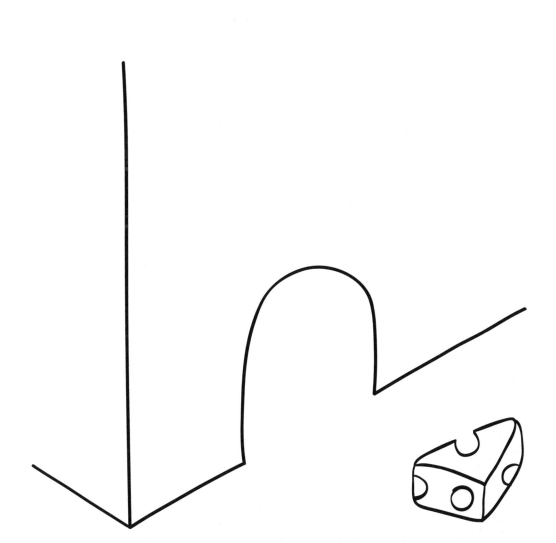

RACCOON

If you give your animal a smile in addition to furrowed eyebrows, it'll look determined!

You can draw a raccoon on all four legs or standing up.

Raccoons are excellent climbers because they can hold on tight. That means they are great huggers too!

Angry

Shy

Shocked

It's expressions time! Draw faces for these blank raccoons: They can be happy, confused, sad, angry, excited, or silly!

RABBIT

Angry

Winking

Thinking

Surprised

This bunny is happily munching on a tasty carrot snack.

Some bunnies have floppy ears, while others have perky ears.

Draw lines behind this bunny to show how fast it's running,
then draw its running buddy underneath.

DOG

Create a fluffy look for your dog with curved lines.

Draw curved lines around your dog's tail to make it look like it's wagging!

This dog has an interesting mouth: round and cute!

The ears you choose for your dog will give it a certain personality. For example, pointy ears make a dog look alert, while droopy ears make a dog look relaxed. See what happens when you draw your dog with these different ear shapes.

Pointed   Curvy   Long   Droopy   Triangular

COW & BULL

Did you know that cows can smell things up to six miles away?

Give your bull a wide stance and angry eyebrows. Look at all that energy!

Here's a cow I drew for you to color! You can choose to color it solid or give it spots. You can add horns and a background too. It's up to you!

Not all cows have spots. And not all cows have horns.

GOAT

Some goats have cute little beards!

Here's a goat with floppy ears. Mix it up with baby horns instead of full-grown ones.

Draw a jumping goat, or make it stand on its hind legs.

Goats have great balance. They can jump very high and run gracefully on mountainsides. Draw another goat jumping from one rock to the next.

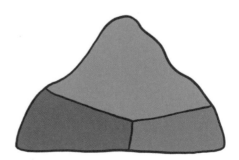

SHEEP

Drawing a sheep is like drawing a fluffy cloud.

Remember that pastel and light colors will always make your drawings more cute.

Draw outstretched arms and legs to show that your sheep is jumping!

If you ever have trouble falling asleep, you can count sheep in your head. Draw sheep in the space above! One sheep, two sheep, three sheep, four sheep... how many little sheep can you fit in?

PIG

Did you know that pigs are actually very clean? They separate where they eat and sleep.

Add the "z"s to show the pig is snoring. It's really enjoying its nap.

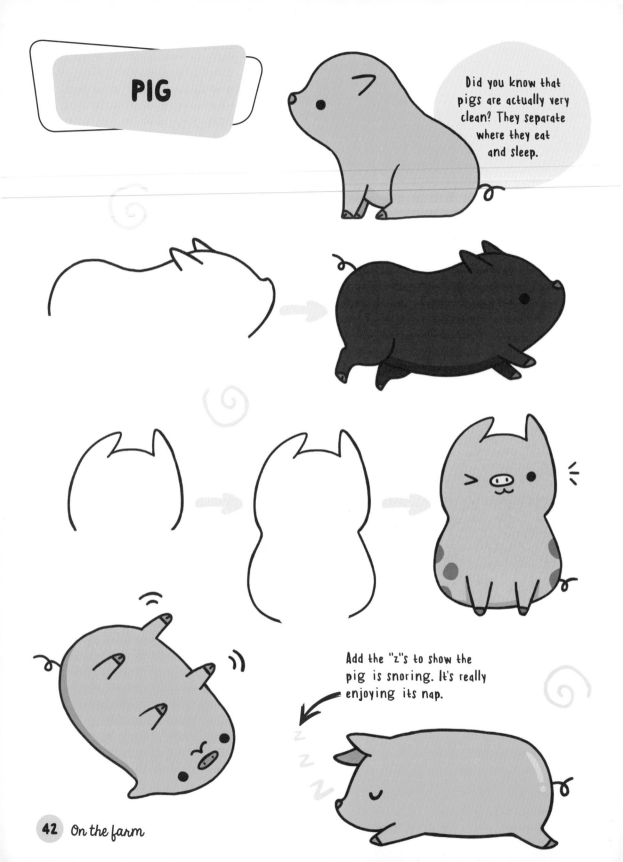

There are so many different colors and patterns
you can choose to decorate your pig. You try!

Spots

Stripes

Zigzags

Swirls

CHICKEN

Drawing a baby chicken is easy; it's like a round yellow ball!

Notice that the chicken is made up of many round strokes.

Roosters are male chickens with very colorful feathers.

This looks like a super-cozy place for a chicken to sit. Draw a mommy chicken keeping her eggs warm.

HORSE

This horse proudly wears its saddle when carrying humans.

Try out this front angle view of a horse. It looks really speedy when you add motion lines.

The direction of the horse's hair can help show which way it is walking.

Horses often have spotty patterns. Sometimes the spots are big and other times they are small. Try some variations on these galloping ponies.

Pick a color for this horse and try to draw large spots.

Now try small spots for this horse! (And pick a different color. Let's mix it up!)

WOLF

In the wild there are red, gray, and white wolves. What color is your favorite wolf?

It feels good to stretch out after a long sleep.

What's that smell? Draw your wolf sniffing for food.

This wolf is howling to the moon. Complete the picture by drawing your own background, not forgetting the moon in the sky!

BEAR

Give your bear a big, round body but itty-bitty ears!

Bears need a lot of body fat to get them through the hibernating months. Draw a really round bear!

This bear is catching fish in the river. Yummy salmon!

Your choice of color will distinguish what type of bear you are drawing: perhaps a polar bear, a grizzly bear, or a panda? Color your own bears to show what type they are.

KANGAROO

Kangaroos have pouches to hold their babies. Baby kangaroos are called joeys.

Kangaroos can travel long distances by hopping. Draw three hopping symbols to show that your kangaroo is on the move.

In this crouching pose, the kangaroo's back is about the same level as the head.

This mama kangaroo is looking at her joey. Draw your own joey to complete the picture. Try to make it look like the joey is looking up at mom.

DEER

I like to add patterns on my deers' backs. Make your own set of dots for your deer.

If you want your deer to have antlers, decide whether they should be short or long.

Long antlers

Short antlers

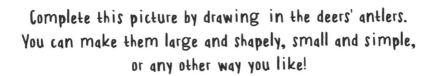

Complete this picture by drawing in the deers' antlers.
You can make them large and shapely, small and simple,
or any other way you like!

OWL

The wingspan of an owl can be incredibly large. Try drawing some owls with their wings open.

I like to add feathers around the page as special effects. Owls can make a mess with all that flapping!

A simple tilt of the head can show so much expression.

Draw some owl friends next to this lonely blue bird. You could even draw one inside the hollow of the tree!

An armadillo's shell is tough, but its underbelly is soft and cuddly.

You can copy this cheerful expression with closed eyes and an open mouth.

Here's a transition of an armadillo rolling up into a ball! Which part is your favorite to draw?

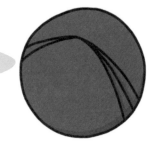

Draw your own walking armadillo below.

Now try drawing an armadillo as it rolls up!

LLAMA

Llamas have soft, thick, fluffy wool to keep them warm.

There are many different llama poses to try. This sitting llama is especially cute.

 Complete this picture by drawing another llama on the left. How cute, two llamas making friends.

BAT

Draw a winking bat, one eye closed and the other open!

Wings are symmetrical, and with practice will become easy to draw.

The bat's dark color camouflages it at night, when it flies around on the hunt for food.

Bats hang upside down when they sleep. Draw a buddy for this bat, both hanging upside down.

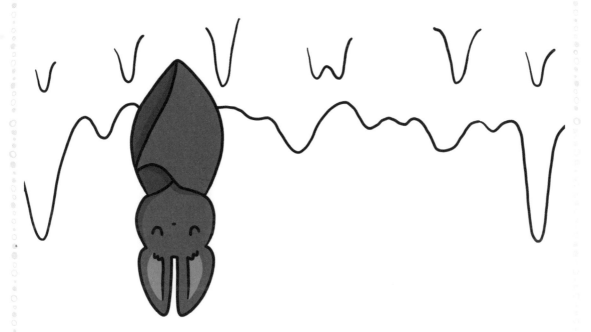

KOALA

Koalas hop from tree to tree in search of their favorite leaves to munch on.

Koala ears are sooooo soft. When drawing them, give them lovely fluffy edges.

A baby koala hangs on to mom's back while it goes looking for food. Draw two baby koalas hitching a ride with their mamas.

RED PANDA

Draw the red panda's tail upward to show that it's jumping. You can really show movement with the tail.

Patterns and colors are what make the red panda so special. Pay attention to the detail in its face and tail.

Give your red panda white eyebrows. Look how much character it has!

Look how happy this red panda is. Draw what you think is making it smile. Is it food, toys, or another panda friend?

CAMEL

Some types of camel have one hump, while others have two.

Camels' humps regulate body temperature, so they can survive in hot climates without much water.

This camel is enjoying a rest. Tuck the back legs in and draw the front legs laid out.

Decide how many humps your camel has before drawing it, so you can proportion the body well.

Camel makeover! Draw your own camel below with a special haircut. Will it be shaggy? Will it be puffy? You decide!

DINOSAURS

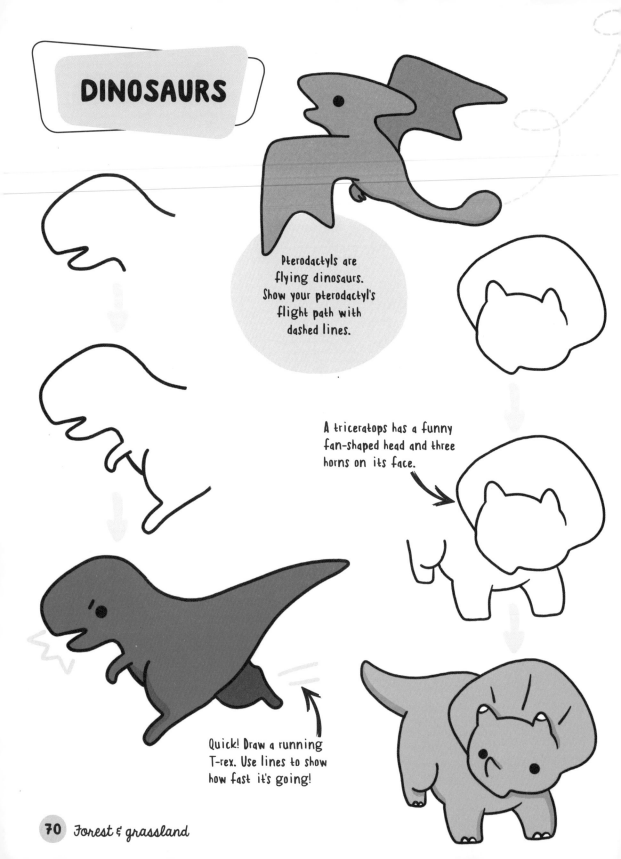

Pterodactyls are flying dinosaurs. Show your pterodactyl's flight path with dashed lines.

A triceratops has a funny fan-shaped head and three horns on its face.

Quick! Draw a running T-rex. Use lines to show how fast it's going!

The dinosaurs on this page are herbivores, meaning they like to eat plants. Draw plants around them so they have something to snack on throughout the day and night.

MONKEY & GORILLA

Give your monkey its favorite food to munch on.

Banana!

Add bumps of fur to make your gorilla look super fuzzy.

Proud, dominant posture

Monkeys can use their tails or legs to hang from trees. Draw more monkeys on this branch. You can make them hang below or sit on top of the branch.

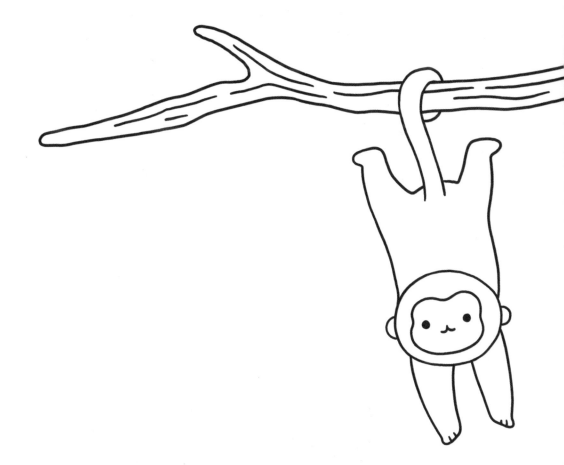

COLORFUL BIRDS

Round beak

Small beak

Long beak

Curved beak

Birds' beaks vary in shape and size. This toucan has an especially large beak.

Drawing a peacock takes patience: you need to repeat the tail feathers over and over.

This cockatoo has a funny feathered hairdo.

What's fun about colorful birds is that you can draw the same outline, but depending on how you color your bird, it will look totally different! Color your own birds below.

ELEPHANT

Drawing an elephant is like drawing a big, fat jelly bean!

Add some tusks to make elephants look both cute and fierce!

An elephant's trunk can show so much emotion. And it can hold many things, like this baby elephant.

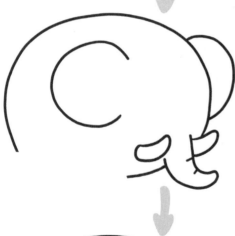

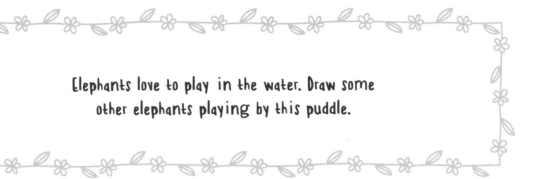

Elephants love to play in the water. Draw some other elephants playing by this puddle.

HIPPO

Draw ripples around the hippo's body to make it look like it's swimming.

The key to drawing a hippo is its square snout but round face.

Hippos can run up to 19 miles per hour on land. That's super fast for an animal that looks slow!

Hippos spend most of their time swimming and napping
in pools. This hippo is having a drink at the water's edge.
Draw in the watering hole, then color in the hippo.

GIRAFFE

Giraffes have long necks so they can reach the delicious leaves high up in the trees.

Draw bending legs to show your giraffe galloping.

Giraffes might look hard to draw because of their patterns. But take it easy and draw the markings one at a time. Start anywhere on this giraffe by drawing a lopsided square. Then draw another square next to your first, and just keep adding on!

Did you know that no two giraffes have the same markings? They are all unique!

LION

Your lion's mane could be thick and full or short and frizzy. It can be large or small, neat or scruffy.

Thick mane

Medium mane

Short mane

The female lion doesn't have a mane. This lady is chilling in the midday sun.

The lion mom is keeping a close watch on her young cubs playing together. But there's only one right now! Draw this cub's brothers and sisters so they can all have fun together.

TIGER

Tigers are like domestic cats. They love to snooze.

A pouncing tiger! Look at the way the paws are turned, like it's ready to jump into a hug!

Stripes on a tiger can seem overwhelming. Just start with the outline of your tiger to keep it simple.

Complete my drawing by adding stripes to the tiger, then draw your own big cat.

SLOTH

Confused

Thinking

Sloths are usually sleepy, but your creations can have all sorts of facial expressions.

Loving

Excited

Sleepy

Sloths use their long claws to hang from tree branches.

Draw a branch for this sloth to hang from. Include leaves on the branch so your sloth can eat them later.

LIZARDS

Chameleons can change colors, so you can draw one again and again, and color it differently every time!

Fins are easy to draw! You can repeat the same shape down the spine of your lizard.

Some lizards have sticky feet that let them climb on walls.

Your lizard's tail can be curly, straight, or curved.

Add details and colors to give these lizards their own style.
Here's a striped one to get you started.

How can you make me look special?

Add fins on the spine of this lizard, or experiment with a spotty pattern.

LEMUR

I made this lemur look fuzzy by drawing rounded patches of fur.

A jumping lemur! Its arms and legs are spread out.

Lemur tails are fun to draw because you can curve them in all sorts of directions.

Lemurs have interesting patterns. Their eyes can be ringed. Their arms and legs might be colored. And their tails are striped. Draw your own lemur below with your choice of patterns!

RHINOCEROS

Drawing the posture and eyes can show how happy your animal is.

Baby rhino

An angry rhino might charge at you! Drawing eyebrows will make your rhino look angry.

Rhinoceroses enjoy bathing in mud! Mud cools their skin and keeps bugs away! Color your own rhino with mud stains to show it's having a great time bathing.

FROG

Draw a jumping frog by making its knees bend!

This is a funny frog. Make its mouth super happy and big!

Adding a lily pad under your frog is a nice finishing touch.

Below are some frog outlines that need your color and pattern expertise! Can you complete the frogs?

Splotchy

Striped

Zigzags

Dotted

WHALE

Use round, curvy lines to draw these gentle creatures.

Whales breathe through their blowholes by puffing out water.

A baby whale is called a calf. They always stay close to their mothers.

Complete this picture! I've drawn the water spurting out of a whale's blowhole. Now you draw the missing whale!

DOLPHIN

Remember, using pastel colors will make your animals even cuter!

This dolphin has a bigger forehead than the other dolphins.

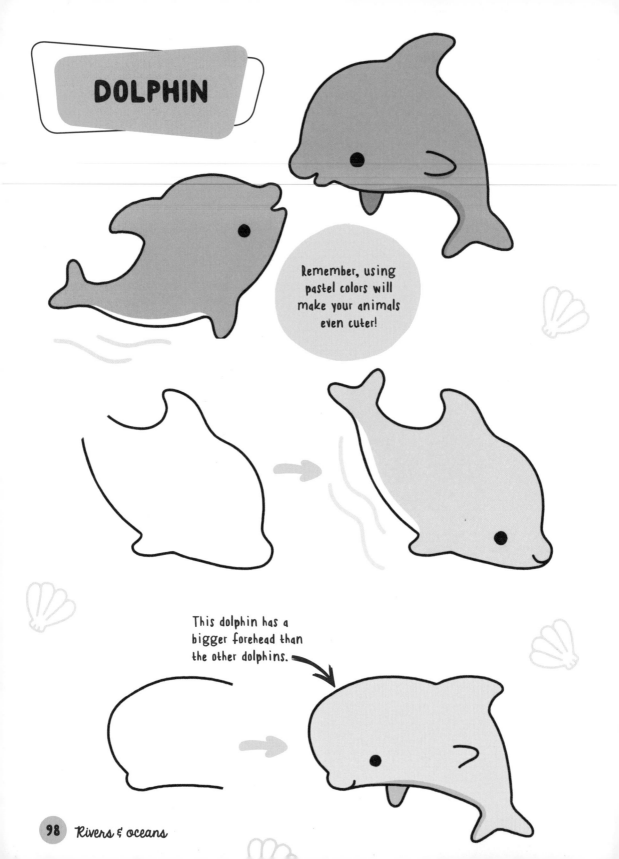

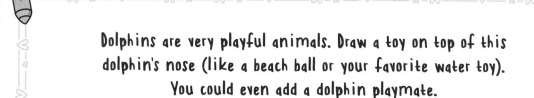

Dolphins are very playful animals. Draw a toy on top of this dolphin's nose (like a beach ball or your favorite water toy). You could even add a dolphin playmate.

FISH

A sun fish is like a large swimming square!

Goldfish can't close their eyes, even when they sleep.

To draw a puffer fish, draw a normal fish and then add spikes.

Patterns can make a fish look difficult to draw. Try drawing the outline first and color in after!

Your choice of color and pattern can change how your fish looks. Here is a school of fish. I've colored some, but the rest are blank for you to complete. You can look at real tropical fish for ideas, or use your imagination to create a whole new species.

PENGUIN

Penguins like to slide on their tummies! Wheeee!

Want to draw a baby and parent penguin? Start by drawing a small one . . .

. . . then draw another penguin, only bigger this time!

Penguins keep their eggs warm between their feet. Color this penguin and its egg to warm them up. In the second drawing, the egg has hatched, so try sketching a penguin chick in place of the egg.

OTTER

Your otter can have so many different expressions!

Angry

Scheming

Nervous

Shocked

Excited

Draw movement lines around your otter to make it float in water.

This otter is running excitedly to its otter family. Draw a group of otters in the space below. If you're up for a challenge, draw them all in different poses!

SHARK

A whale shark has a round, fat body type.

Pointy teeth and angry eyebrows make a shark look vicious.

It is not too surprising that a hammerhead shark has a head that looks like a hammer!

Give these sharks their own color and pattern combinations.
Try solid colors, stripes, spots, or mixed colors!

CRAB & LOBSTER

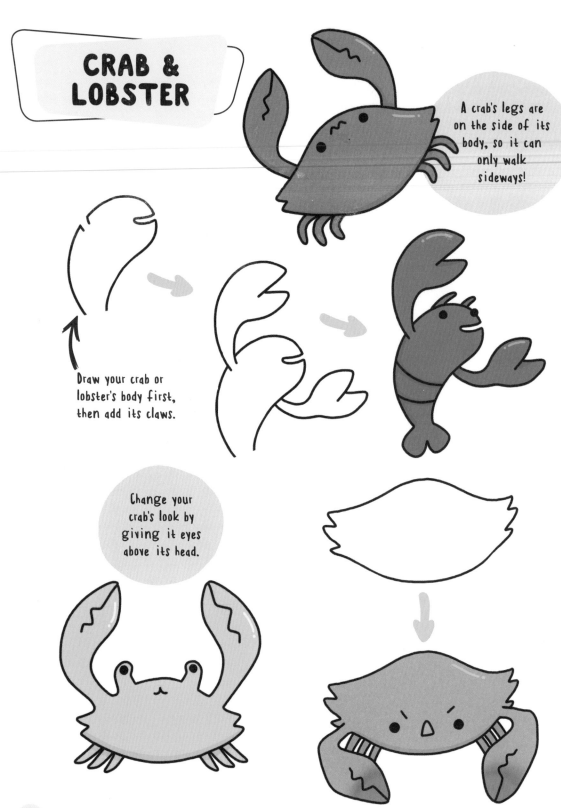

A crab's legs are on the side of its body, so it can only walk sideways!

Draw your crab or lobster's body first, then add its claws.

Change your crab's look by giving it eyes above its head.

You might find a crab on sand, under water, or even in the jungle. Draw your own environment for this crab. Don't forget to add a crab buddy. We don't want a lonely crustacean!

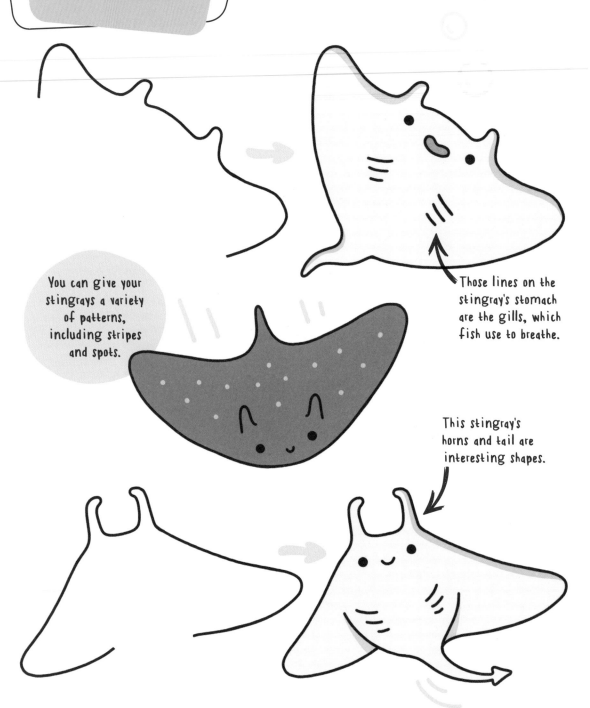

You can give your stingrays a variety of patterns, including stripes and spots.

Those lines on the stingray's stomach are the gills, which fish use to breathe.

This stingray's horns and tail are interesting shapes.

Trace over the tails and horns below to practice, then draw your own. They can be short, long, curved, or straight. Don't forget to give your stingrays some interesting patterning on their bodies.

SEAL

Start drawing your seal with a lumpy head.

Upside-down seal is waving hello! It's laying on its back.

Some seals have large spots in one area, while others are speckled all over with little spots.

Give each of these contented seals a completely different
pattern or color palette.

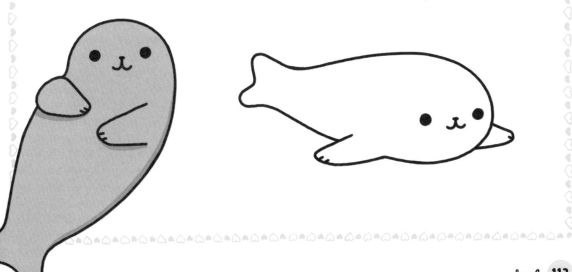

SEAHORSE

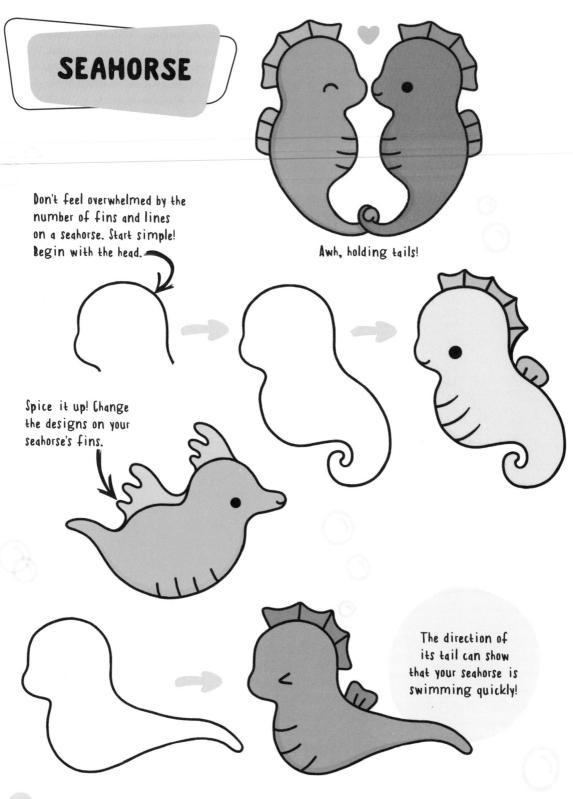

Awh, holding tails!

Don't feel overwhelmed by the number of fins and lines on a seahorse. Start simple! Begin with the head.

Spice it up! Change the designs on your seahorse's fins.

The direction of its tail can show that your seahorse is swimming quickly!

Draw your own family of seahorses. Make them colorful, and give them different fins and tails. Most important, have fun!

I drew this one just for you.

WALRUS

Walruses have long teeth called tusks!

It's really easy to add whiskers to your walrus. Just draw a few short straight lines!

This walrus is laying flat on its belly. Tuck its flippers neatly by its side.

Complete this drawing! Give the walrus tusks, whiskers, and flippers. Then color him in and add your choice of background.

OCTOPUS & SQUID

Their sticky tentacles mean octopuses can cling onto rocks and plants.

Squid are so fun to draw. Begin by drawing their bodies, then add the arms!

Draw some octopuses hanging out on the big and small rocks.
Add some squid swimming around and plants on the ocean floor.
Soon you'll have a complete ocean environment.

NARWHAL

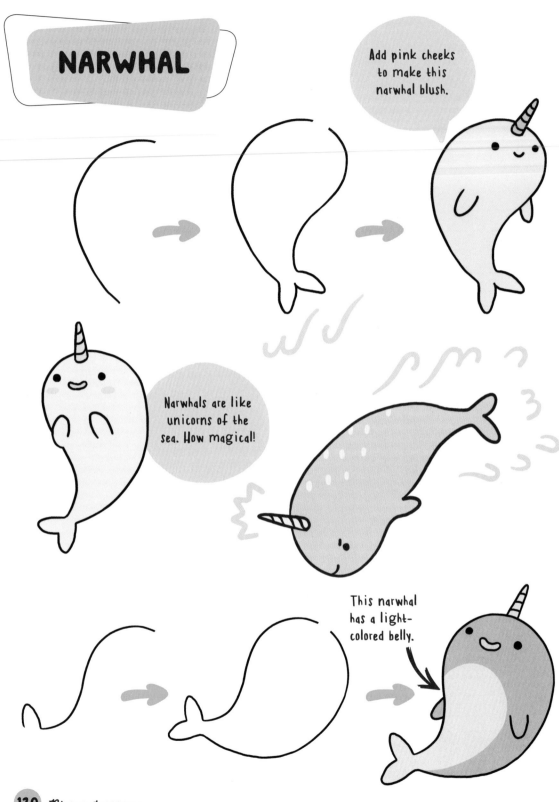

Add pink cheeks to make this narwhal blush.

Narwhals are like unicorns of the sea. How magical!

This narwhal has a light-colored belly.

There are so many different colors and patterns you can choose to decorate your narwhal. Draw and color your own designs below.

BEAVER

Beavers are so round. Imagine drawing two circles: one for the head and another for the body.

A beaver's front teeth never stop growing! They gnaw on wood to keep them short.

This is a silly beaver sitting on its round tail.

Beavers collect branches and sticks to create houses by the river. Complete this home by drawing more sticks inside the dotted lines. You could draw in another beaver to help out. Teamwork!

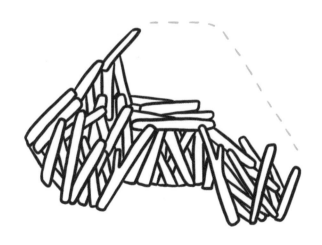

TURTLE

When drawing turtles, start with the head, then position the shell behind it.

Different shell angles

Try drawing a turtle hiding in its shell. Its eyes are peering out at you!

Turtles like to eat vegetables and fru

Shell patterns are unique to every turtle. Create your own patterns and colors for these four turtles.

PLATYPUS

Platypus' flipper arms and big tails make them great swimmers.

Notice that the mouth is the same round shape as the tail.

Achoo! This platypus just sneezed! Do you see that silly expression on its face?

Here's an environment I drew for you. Draw some platypus underwater or on land. You pick!

CREDITS

AUTHOR ACKNOWLEDGMENTS

My art career couldn't have launched without the support of my parents. Mom and Dad, thanks for encouraging me since Day 1 that my art could inspire the world. You still saw talent in me even though I had annoying urges like coloring on our white walls (which you made me clean up afterward).